Strengthen Your Most Intimate Relationship

7 SECRETS TO AN AWESOME MARRIAGE

DISCUSSION GUIDE

KIM KIMBERLING, PhD

Foreward by Craig & Amy Groeschel

7 Secrets to an Awesome Marriage Discussion Guide
© 2015 Kim Kimberling

ISBN 978-0692498279

http://www.iwantanawesomemarriage.com/

SESSION 1

Have each person read "A First Word" before meeting together.

https://youtu.be/wWtweH2NFGs

A FIRST WORD:

If you are married, think back on your wedding day. Would you do it all over again? The odds seem so stacked against us, don't they? Every year many more divorces occur than marriages. More people today are living together and not marrying—just kicking the tires, or something like that. And shockingly, more couples are choosing to divorce before they celebrate their first anniversary than ever before.

We live in this world that gives us more good reasons to not marry than to marry. Unmarried people witness the struggles married people face—porn and affairs and all the other things that stack up against marriage—and often conclude that avoiding marriage is their best option. It seems that many people have just thrown marriage under the bus.

Yet I talk to people every day who still hold on to the dream that marriage is for them. Maybe some of them are idealistic, but they live for their dream to come true.

Today I am amazed to see more couples in the counseling room than ever before where one or both have had an affair or participated in some type of infidelity. That may not surprise you, but I think this will: I see more and more people willing to fight for their affair-scarred marriages than ever before. Maybe they understand that affairs don't fulfill the promises that they make. Maybe they are aware that less than 1% of marriages that start out of an affair make it. Maybe they figured out that what they had was a lot better than what they were pursuing. Maybe.

So, would I get married again? I know you are thinking: He has to say yes; after all, he is a Christian marriage counselor. If I am going to have any credibility with you at all, I have to be honest. So my answer is yes—not because it is the "right" thing for me to say, but because from the depths of my heart, I love being married to Nancy. She has been my constant companion since she was eighteen. We kind of grew up together. We had to figure things out. We brought baggage into our marriage that we should have checked long before we did. We had to learn new ways to connect and to stay connected and how to fight together instead of fighting each other. We had to balance life so it did not overwhelm us. And sex, that was a whole other battle. But do you know what really made the difference? Do you know what really helped me be able to say I would do this marriage thing all over again? We had to make the choice to put God in our marriage—not on the outside or a little bit inside, but all the way in. God had to be number one.

You see, what we learned was that we didn't need to have all the answers, because God did. That doesn't mean that our life has been perfect, because it hasn't. What it does mean is that we discovered that God loved us and valued our marriage more than we could have ever imagined. He created it. He designed it, and He had this perfect plan for our marriage. He also has a perfect plan for yours. So what do you do? What is your job? Follow Him. Follow Him as individuals, and follow Him as a couple.

In this series, we're going to look at how to do just that. We'll look at seven secrets that can dramatically change your marriage. Then it will be your choice. What will you do with them?

ICE BREAKER FOR SMALL GROUPS:

Have each couple share how they met, how long they dated, their "proposal story," and how long they have been married.

QUESTIONS:

1. Dr. Kim talked about things that stack up against marriage. What are some of the things you see that attack marriages today? How do you think a couple should deal with them?

_____

_____

_____

_____

_____

_____

2. What can you do as a couple to keep your marriage from being "thrown under the bus"?

_____

_____

_____

_____

_____

3. Rate as a couple where you think you put God in your marriage today (1–10, with 10 being the highest). Is He number one or two or ten or not on your radar? Honestly, where do you want Him to be? What would be a first step in making that happen?

_____

_____

_____

_____

_____

4. What is one expectation that you have for your marriage in doing this study?

_____

_____

_____

_____

PRAYER:

FOR A SMALL GROUP:

Allow each person to share something relating to today's session that they would like the group to pray about for them. Have one person close in prayer. (It is essential that each person in the group holds things shared in the group in the strictest of confidence.)

FOR A COUPLE:

Pray that God will grow your marriage as you do this study together.

HOMEWORK:

Read "Secret Number 1: STOP."

SESSION 2

STOP: The Insanities That Hold Us Back

https://youtu.be/E4q5q0J_OBk

When you hear the word insanity, what comes to your mind? Maybe a character from a movie you saw sometime in the past or a decision you saw someone make and thought to yourself, "That is totally insane."

A well-known description of the word insanity is doing the same thing over and over again and expecting a different result every time. Think about this scenario: I get ready to leave the house for work one day and discover when I try to start my car that the battery is dead. So I go back in the house and sit in my chair, and every thirty minutes I go back in the garage and try to start the car. I do that over and over all morning. That is insanity—doing the same thing over and over expecting different results. For my car to start, I have to do something different. I need to call someone to come and charge the battery or replace it. My car will not start until one of those two actions is successfully carried out.

We all have our little insanities. Most of them are harmless and affect no one but ourselves. But what about the insanities we have in marriage? Are they harmless? Do they just affect us and no one else?

I grew up with great parents who had an incredible marriage, which served as the ideal model for me. So when Nancy and I got married, I tried to fit her into the same mold as my mother. My logical thinking went something like this: My mother was a great wife; Nancy wanted to be a great wife; so Nancy needed to be like my mom. Made perfect sense to me. That was my expectation. Now, there were two big things wrong with this expectation: (1) Nancy wasn't my mom and did not want to be, and (2) I was not going to be able to "force" her into anything. My insanity was that I continued to hold Nancy to this unreasonable expectation over and over and over again in the first years of our marriage.

What about you? What expectations do you have in your marriage? Are they realistic? Have you shared them with your spouse? Honestly, my expectation of Nancy was unrealistic. There wasn't anything wrong in wanting her to be a great wife (she wanted to be a great wife too), but the problem was that I wanted to define Nancy according to who my mom was and how my mom interacted with my dad as a wife. The really crazy part was that I never shared this expectation with Nancy, yet I became angry with her when she didn't meet that unrealistic and unspoken expectation. Insanity? Oh, yeah! That was me.

Now would be a great time to take a deeper look at your marriage. What are your expectations? Are they realistic or not? Have you shared them? Have they turned into insanities? If you rated your marriage on a one-to-ten scale, where would you rate it? Where would you want it to be in five years? Ten years? What do you need to do today to have the marriage you want today and tomorrow?

The first step to change is always the hardest, but nothing will ever change until you take that first step. Don't let something stand in the way of having the marriage God has for you. Stopping the insanity is your first secret.

ICE BREAKER FOR SMALL GROUPS:

Have each person share a pet peeve that they have.

QUESTIONS:

1. What is something in your life that would fall into Dr. Kim's definition of insanity? How does it affect your marriage?

_____

_____

_____

_____

_____

_____

_____

_____

2. Name one expectation that you brought into marriage that you did not share with your spouse ahead of time? How has that affected your marriage?

_____

_____

_____

_____

_____

_____

_____

3. What makes an expectation realistic or unrealistic?

_____

_____

_____

_____

_____

4. Rate your marriage on the 1–10 scale (with 10 being the best). Then rate it where you would like it to be in one year. What do you need to do each day to have the marriage you want in a year?

_____

_____

_____

_____

_____

PRAYER:

FOR A SMALL GROUP:

Allow each person to share something relating to today's session that they would like the group to pray about for them. Have one person close in prayer. (It is essential that each person in the group holds things shared in the group in the strictest of confidence.)

FOR A COUPLE:

As you agree on things to do to improve your marriage over the next year, pray for God's wisdom, strength, and help as you move your marriage forward.

HOMEWORK:

1. Make a list of the expectations you have in your marriage today, and then answer these questions:

_____

_____

_____

_____

_____

a. Are your expectations realistic or not?

_____

_____

_____

_____

_____

b. Have you shared your expectations with your spouse?

_____

_____

_____

_____

_____

c. Have any of your expectations turned into insanities?

_____

_____

_____

_____

_____

d. Share your answers with your spouse.

_____

_____

_____

_____

_____

2. Read "Secret Number 2: START."

SESSION 3

START: The Practice of Putting God First, Spouse Second

https://youtu.be/OY9RC8WbBt0

As far back as I can remember, I knew about God. Our family was in church and Sunday school every week. I knew all the Bible stories and the songs that went with them.

My granddad was a man of God, and he was my hero. Honestly, I thought I had that whole God thing nailed down. God and I were tight. I think I understood faith as good as an eleven-year-old could understand it. I even thought I would be a pastor someday. It was awesome.

Then I entered puberty. My body began to change. More than that, the girl down the block—who used to ride bikes and shoot baskets with me—began to change too. I was confused. What had seemed so easy suddenly seemed really difficult for me.

I was on a roller-coaster ride with God that continued through middle school and high school. Sometimes I had it nailed down, and sometimes I was confused. Then came college life, and other than going to church when I was at home on school breaks, I put God on a shelf somewhere in my life.

It was halfway through my junior year of college that I met Nancy and my life changed—not overnight, but over the next two years. I knew I had to find God again. I was falling in love with this woman and was thinking about marriage. Somewhere deep inside, I knew God had to be a part of it. Nancy felt the same way. We agreed to look for a church that we both liked; other than that, we had no idea where to begin. We knew we needed to put Him first in our lives, but putting Him first in our marriage was a mystery. Uncovering that mystery became a process for us.

What about you? You and God? You and God and your marriage? Where is He in your life today? Where is He in your marriage?

Please, listen to me closely here. We are all from different spiritual backgrounds. The last thing I want is for you to make a checklist of all you need to do to put God in your marriage. Including

Him in your marriage doesn't require a checklist. It is not about what you are supposed to do and not do. It has to do with one thing and one thing only: your heart. Love Him with everything—your entire being—and then invite Him into your marriage. Give Him the steering wheel of your life and marriage. Follow His lead. Trust Him. Seek Him. When you do that, He will build your marriage into something far greater than you ever dreamed or expected! The bottom line is that you have a choice: to allow God in or leave God out. What will you choose?

ICE BREAKER FOR SMALL GROUPS:

Have each person share about the person that has had the greatest spiritual influence on their life.

QUESTIONS:

1. During what time in your life has it been most difficult to stay connected to God? Why?

_____

_____

_____

_____

_____

2. Where is God in your marriage today? Where do you want Him to be?

_____

_____

_____

_____

_____

3. Why is Dr. Kim so adamant that growing together spiritually doesn't require a "checklist"?

_____

_____

_____

_____

_____

4. What will you commit to begin to do this week that will either put God in your marriage or let Him in further than you ever have before?

_____

_____

_____

_____

_____

PRAYER:

FOR A SMALL GROUP:

Allow each person to share something relating to today's session that they would like the group to pray about for them. Have one person close in prayer. (It is essential that each person in the group holds things shared in the group in the strictest of confidence.)

FOR A COUPLE:

Pray for God to change your hearts as you allow Him to take control of your marriage.

HOMEWORK:

Read "Secret Number 3: CONNECT."

SESSION 4

CONNECT: The Art of Listening and Being Present

https://youtu.be/NXXbUQZe3Jk

As a counselor, I see couples in all kinds of different situations. Someone recently asked me what marriage issues bother me the most. If I really think about it, I am most troubled by couples who just exist together. You've seen some of them. In fact, it can actually happen to any of us if we don't work at connecting. Most of these couples don't fight. They just live their lives like roommates. It's as if they are in a business deal together. They're cordial to each other. They may eat a few meals together each week and sit in front of the same TV watching the same show occasionally. They may even laugh at the same things. But their relationship subsists only on the surface. They never talk about feelings or emotions. They may have sex a few times a week, month, or year, but it is little more than a physical act. If one gets sick, the other will probably help them. Maybe. It's a marriage of convenience—but not too convenient. Unfortunately, they are missing out on the greatest gift, next to Jesus, that God has given us. They have chosen to coexist instead of connecting in their marriage.

In our marriage we had times when we simply existed together. We weren't connecting. The distractions of life got in the way of our marriage. We all have distractions. Some are good and some are not. Some are absolutely necessary and some are absolutely not. Here's an example that may upset some of you. Most of us would agree that the greatest gift that God gives us in our marriages is children. But guess what? Children are a distraction. They take time and energy. Most couples see a change in how connected they feel when children come. If they don't get proactive and creative in connecting, they can slowly drift apart.

Then there is the busyness of life. It may be work, or serving at church, or a sport, or a thousand other things that we get involved in. Many of these are good things until they have a negative effect on our marriage. When that happens, something needs to change. What happens when you are distracted? Think about it this way: You are always communicating something to your spouse, whether you are talking or being silent. You are constantly communicating, but what are you communicating? Are you communicating how important your spouse is to you or how far down on your list they are? Are you connecting or disconnecting? Are you intentionally showing your spouse that they are the most important thing in your life next to God or not? Are you growing closer together or further apart?

If you are connected, keep it up. My experience is that you can't just get connected and stop working on it. It is something you have to do day after day after day.

If you are not connected, stop here. Don't go any further until you sit down together and make a plan to connect. Depending on how unconnected you are, you may need the help of someone in your small group, or a pastor, or a Christian counselor. Just don't put it off any longer. Whatever it takes, do it—and do it now!

ICE BREAKER FOR SMALL GROUPS:

Have each couple share something their spouse does for them that shows love.

QUESTIONS:

1. We can all have times in our marriage when we just exist. How would you know if that was happening or has happened in your marriage?

_____

_____

_____

_____

_____

2. Have each person name a distraction in their life that can take away from their marriage.

_____

_____

_____

_____

_____

3. If you showed everyone in your group your weekly calendar, what would it say about your priorities?

_____

_____

_____

_____

_____

4. If you are connected, what one thing do you need to keep doing to stay connected? If you are not connected today, what is your first step to begin to create a connection?

_____

_____

_____

_____

_____

_____

PRAYER:

FOR A SMALL GROUP:

Allow each person to share something relating to today's session that they would like the group to pray about for them. Have one person close in prayer. (It is essential that each person in the group holds things shared in the group in the strictest of confidence.)

FOR A COUPLE:

Pray for God to help you keep Him first and each other second each day.

HOMEWORK:

Read "Secret Number 4: ENGAGE."

SESSION 5

ENGAGE: How to Fight Right

https://youtu.be/CRc3QNKDYBw

I hate it when Nancy and I fight. We both hate it. Thankfully, today we fight very little. But you would never have guessed that we hated fighting from some of the fights we had in the first few years of our marriage. They would escalate quickly, and we would say things we later regretted. When we fought, we both wanted to win. Winning in a marriage is never good unless both partners win. But that wasn't our goal. Our fights ended with one winner and one loser, and our marriage was sinking.

Almost everything I tell couples not to do, we did. In counseling sessions, I stress to couples how important it is to choose your battles in marriage. There are so many things that could cause an argument, and it is so important to not fight about everything. But we fought about everything. At times it probably looked like we were inventing things to fight about.

What took us a really long time to learn was that we didn't have to continue fighting this way. In reality, we would never see everything eye to eye. We were going to have conflict, but no one ever told us that we could disagree in a healthy way. For us, fight meant fight.

When we finally learned that we could fight right or fight wrong, it seemed like the heavens parted. We discovered that instead of using negative and hurtful words, we could use positive and healing words. This became a turning point for our marriage. We learned to engage. We learned how to fight right.

What about you and your marriage? How do you fight? What are the words you say? How do you say them? Fighting right takes more time and creative energy than fighting wrong. But fighting right—engaging—can grow your marriage. It can draw you closer together. It can give you the confidence that with God's help, there is nothing you can't conquer as a couple. If you think you need a miracle so you can engage instead of fight, I have great news. We have a God who is truly full of miracles, and He has one for you. Just ask Him!

ICE BREAKER FOR SMALL GROUPS:

Have each couple share something they argued about in the past that seems trivial today.

QUESTIONS:

1. When you hear the word conflict, what comes to your mind?

_____

_____

_____

_____

_____

2. What word would you use to describe how you and your spouse fight in your marriage?

_____

_____

_____

_____

_____

3. What does Dr. Kim mean when he says, "Winning in a marriage is never good unless both partners win"?

_____

_____

_____

_____

_____

4. As a couple, what would help you make the transition from fighting to engaging?

_____

_____

_____

_____

_____

PRAYER:

FOR A SMALL GROUP:

Allow each person to share something relating to today's session that they would like the group to pray about for them. Have one person close in prayer. (It is essential that each person in the group holds things shared in the group in the strictest of confidence.)

FOR A COUPLE:

Pray for God to help you choose your battles well and engage instead of fight wrong in your disagreements.

HOMEWORK:

Read "Secret Number 5: BALANCE."

SESSION 6

BALANCE: Scheduling for a Better Marriage

https://youtu.be/fXdyWntRAXA

How's your balance? Mine has always been pretty good. I learned to ride a bike when I was really young. Then growing up I conquered my skateboard and mastered both snow skiing and waterskiing. Every time I went to the circus as a kid, I felt sure that I could walk a tightrope just like the circus stars, if given the chance.

Balance is very important. It can mean the difference between standing up or falling down. Balance within a marriage is crucial.

For a marriage to be in balance, each person needs to be in balance. With physical balance, Nancy standing upright has nothing to do with whether I fall or not. But if my life gets out of balance, that's different. It affects her; and the more I am out of balance, the more it hurts our marriage.

Here's an example. I get really excited about what I do. I love working with people in the counseling room. I love teaching at live events. I love creating videos and writing and helping people through Christian coaching. I love leading Awesome Marriage. The problem comes when all those things that I love to do cause me to get out of balance with Nancy. Since her love language is quality time, things can get out of balance rather quickly when I'm not intentional about spending time with her. At this point in our marriage, I'm a whole lot better at recognizing when that happens than I used to be, but I still have to work at it.

What about you? Where can you get out of balance, and how does that affect your spouse? What about your marriage? What do you need to do to bring balance to it? In the book, I talk about a number of ways to add balance to your marriage. Look those over and use them as a guide or even a checklist. What are you doing and what are you not doing? Then together pick one idea, and commit to focus on it together as a couple. Think it through together. When will you start? Are there any obstacles that you need to deal with first? Then go. Work hard together to bring balance into your marriage.

Once you have successfully brought one new balance idea into your marriage, pick another one to work on. Actually the whole secret of working together to add balance to your marriage goes back to one of the foundational principles that we have talked about before: God first, spouse second. If you hold fast to that principle, then adding balance is another secret that will take your marriage to a new level.

ICE BREAKER FOR SMALL GROUPS:

Have each person share a time when they "lost their balance."

QUESTIONS:

1. What are some of the ways that a marriage can get out of balance?

_____

_____

_____

_____

_____

2. What in your life is out of balance? What do you need to do to bring your life into balance?

_____

_____

_____

_____

_____

3. What have you done as a couple to bring balance into your marriage?

_____

_____

_____

4. In the book, Dr. Kim talks about a number of ways to add balance to your marriage. What is one you can work on together, and how do you see it helping your marriage?

_____

_____

_____

_____

_____

PRAYER:

FOR A SMALL GROUP:

Allow each person to share something relating to today's session that they would like the group to pray about for them. Have one person close in prayer. (It is essential that each person in the group holds things shared in the group in the strictest of confidence.)

FOR A COUPLE:

Ask God for wisdom in discovering ways to help each other create more balance in your marriage.

HOMEWORK:

Read "Secret Number 6: MINGLE."

SESSION 7

MINGLE: Sex as the Mingling of Souls

https://youtu.be/U1YxLjyhjpk

Today we live in a society that considers itself sexually liberated— very open about all things concerning sex. A paradox I have found with this is that I see very few couples who actually talk together about their sex life. Our culture generates magazine or blog articles on "12 new ways to please your man" and "14 new ways to drive your woman wild" yet takes us further and further away from "great sex." If one of these "top 10 ways" really worked, there wouldn't be a need for the next magazine issue or blog post touting a new set of ten or twelve or whatever number of ways to do whatever. Would it?

If I were to pick out twenty couples and invite them to a workshop on sex and ask them to recommend a good book or article on sex that we could reference during the workshop, what do you think they would you say? Something from a men's or women's magazine or another best-selling book? Very few, if any, people would say, "The Bible." In fact, if I announced to the twenty couples at the beginning of the workshop that our text would be the Bible, I am pretty sure I would hear a collective groan! Maybe some would politely remain quiet but silently groan nevertheless. The most common question would be why? Why the Bible?

Let's back up. Somewhere in the events of creation, God created sex. Now think through this with me. Who gave a man and a woman their sex organs? Who designed the sensitive nerves that provide incredible pleasure? Who made us so that in sex we fit perfectly together? God. He made man and woman and had this great idea about sex. It wasn't supposed to be something dirty or nasty, but beautiful. I think God was very excited to give us that gift and to see us receive it.

There's a book in the Bible called the Song of Solomon, which gives us a really sexy picture of a husband and his wife enjoying each other. Twice the man and woman make love. One time he starts at her head and moves down her body; another time he starts at her feet and moves up her body. The Bible says they enjoyed each other all night long.

Sex was God's plan. He provided a way for the physical, emotional, and spiritual to all come together and mingle in one amazing act. Wow! This was His gift to us. Yet somehow we've messed it up. I want you to experience sex exactly the way God intended it to be enjoyed. It is going to take some more work. You may need healing from the past. You may need to flush out all the distorted sexual crud that our culture has fed you. You may even need to go back to square one and start over. It's possible that you will need help. That's okay. Get it. There's nothing to be ashamed of. Once your baggage from the past has been checked, you will experience sex in a way you never dreamed possible.

I say it all the time, but I believe it with all that I am: The best sex ever can only happen in the context of a Christian marriage. Don't ever settle for less.

ICE BREAKER FOR SMALL GROUPS:

Have each person share where they first learned about sex.

QUESTIONS:

1. What are some of the messages that our culture gives us about sex and sexuality?

_____

_____

_____

_____

_____

2. When we stop and think that God is really the One who invented sex, how can that change the way we look at the sexual relationship between a husband and a wife?

_____

_____

_____

_____

3. To keep your marriage pure in a sexually liberated culture, what are the constraints you need to put in place in your lives and in your marriage?

_____

_____

_____

_____

_____

4. Dr. Kim says that the best sex ever can only happen in the context of a Christian marriage. What does that mean to you?

_____

_____

_____

_____

_____

PRAYER:

FOR A SMALL GROUP:

Allow each person to share something relating to today's session that they would like the group to pray about for them. Have one person close in prayer. (It is essential that each person in the group holds things shared in the group in the strictest of confidence.)

FOR A COUPLE:

Pray together for God's protection over your marriage.

HOMEWORK:

Read "Secret Number 7: FIGHT."

FIGHT: The Power of Fighting Together on the Same Team

https://youtu.be/LoRtiFVU9vI

In order for Nancy and me to quit fighting each other and begin fighting together, we needed a change in our stance. Instead of standing face to face yelling at each other, we pivoted so we could stand side by side yelling together at something else. A simple pivot changed our marriage.

We learned that when we were fighting each other, God was usually nowhere to be found. We weren't calling on Him or honoring Him with our actions or our words. I think He probably found something else to do besides watching us fight. But when we began fighting together, He was there. He was right there with us to help us, to encourage us, and to give us answers that we never would have found on our own.

What about you? Are you fighting each other or fighting together? Think about your money—the number one thing couples fight about. What if instead of arguing about money or how you spend it, you prayed together about your finances? What would happen if you created a budget together and maybe even took a finance class together? That is fighting together. That is fighting on the same team.

Marriage is not easy, and fighting each other only complicates the situation. It seems that it's easy for us to fall into patterns of fighting that we hate but keep repeating over and over and over. And with each repeat, we knock another hole in the foundation of our marriage.

I plead with couples to fight together, to break bad cycles, to love each other like Christ loves us. Often, however, my words seem to fall on deaf ears. I beg you, don't let that be you. Make the choice to not only be on the same team but also act like you are on the same team. Most importantly, make room for God on your team.

Learning to fight together with God on your team takes a marriage that is losing and replaces it with a marriage that is winning. That is really cool!

ICE BREAKER FOR SMALL GROUPS:

Have each couple share a time when they fought together.

QUESTIONS:

1. What does making a "pivot" mean to you when potential conflict comes up?

_____

_____

_____

_____

_____

2. What does Dr. Kim mean when he says that when he and Nancy fought, God was usually nowhere to be found?

_____

_____

_____

_____

_____

3. Discuss topics in marriage that couples fight about. What does it mean for a couple to choose their battles?

_____

_____

_____

_____

_____

4. What step or steps do you need to take for you, your spouse, and God to always fight together on the same team?

_____

_____

_____

_____

_____

PRAYER:

FOR A SMALL GROUP:

Allow each person to share something relating to today's session that they would like the group to pray about for them. Have one person close in prayer. (It is essential that each person in the group holds things shared in the group in the strictest of confidence.)

FOR A COUPLE:

Pray that God would teach you as a couple how to fight together on the same team.

HOMEWORK:

Read "A FINAL WORD."

SESSION 9

A FINAL WORD

https://youtu.be/EA28XJsgwD0

It's time to wrap this up. My prayer is that your marriage is better today than it was when you began this study. If divorce was on the table, I hope it's now off. If your marriage was a 2, I hope it's a 4 or 5 or more. If your marriage was a 7, I hope it's an 8 or 9 or 10.

But don't miss this: Wherever you were and wherever you are today, don't stop. Having an Awesome Marriage is not completing a nine-part study and then coasting the rest of your life. Having an Awesome Marriage takes work every day, but the payoff for all the hard work is amazing!

Think back through the secrets. Where are you with each of them?

Have you identified the insanities in your marriage? What about taking steps to STOP them?

Where are you in STARTING to pursue God together? Are you praying together?

Are you setting aside enough time to really CONNECT and then using that time wisely?

How about ENGAGING in a way that grows your marriage instead of tearing it apart? Are you on board with that?

Have you found BALANCE that works for you, your spouse, and God?

What about your sex life? Are you taking the time to MINGLE and have the best sex ever?

Which way are you facing while you FIGHT? Are you still facing each other and fighting it out or standing side by side as you face everything that life throws at you?

Secrets are intriguing, but secrets are no more than words until we turn them into action. The formula for having an Awesome Marriage is simple: Turn the secrets into steps. The work is hard; it is a one-day-at-a-time deal, over and over and over. But never forget that the God of the universe is always on your side.

ICE BREAKER FOR SMALL GROUPS:

Have each couple share where they think their marriage is today versus where it was at the beginning of the course.

QUESTIONS:

1. Which "secret" has had the greatest impact on your marriage so far? How?

_____

_____

_____

_____

_____

2. Which "secret" is God now leading you to turn into a step? Why is this "secret" important to the health of your marriage?

_____

_____

_____

_____

_____

3. What do you need to do as a couple to continue to build your own Awesome Marriage?

_____

_____

_____

_____

_____

4. What are some ways that you can now impact other marriages for God?

_____

_____

_____

_____

_____

PRAYER:

FOR A SMALL GROUP:

Allow each person to share something relating to today's session that they would like the group to pray about for them. Have one person close in prayer. (It is essential that each person in the group holds things shared in the group in the strictest of confidence.)

FOR A COUPLE:

Pray together that God would guide you as you turn these secrets into steps in your marriage.

A FINAL WORD FROM DR. KIM:

I am excited to learn how God is working in your marriage and would love for you to communicate that to us. I invite you to join us every day on our Awesome Marriage social media sites, our YouTube channel, and our website. We have tons of free videos, posts, ideas, and blogs that will encourage you and help you as you, your spouse, and God develop your own Awesome Marriage.

31921846R00020